Cradle of Song

Priscilla Mileski

BookLeaf Publishing

India | USA | UK

Presentation by *BookLeaf Publishing*

Web: www.bookleafpub.com

E-mail: info@bookleafpub.com

ISBN: 9789363313798

First edition 2024

To the curious, the lovers of nature and the poets.

ACKNOWLEDGEMENT

Thank you to my editor, Madeline and to all who encouraged me.

PREFACE

Pause and savor each moment, everyone of them has importance and meaning.

The Muse

The Muse is my lover now
demanding and delightful.
Again and again
she urges my dreams
and my hand to witness life
through small crystal balls.

Words roll like marbles
off the edge of my tongue.

Summer Evenings

Warm summer
evenings on the porch
we listened to the
songs of coyotes.

The long notes
echoed in the valleys
between ancient
worn down mountains.

The dogs by our side
would join in
for a measure,
wistful as fog.

False Light

Misinformation
brings disorientation
as the moth orbits
a moonless light in a
frenzied flight
of self-regulation.

Summer blooms
and a planetary world
suffer the loss
of moon-lit pollination.

Beltane

Words written
on both bay leaf
and rose petal float
for a moment on the rising heat of fire.

Ribbon tied bundles
of river birch
crackle and snap.
They blaze into
a reach of yellow flame.

Evening birds rustle and sigh softly
before their deep sleep,
while the thin white smoke
summons the starry light
of the seven sisters.

Catbird Cradle

Catbird sits on the pole
and watches me
through the window.
He lets me know he has
returned from the Gulf.
He rebuilds last year's nest
in the same bush.

This, this singular
place in all the world
is the cradle of his song,
his inspired lineage.
The navigation of his
fierce and fragile life
balanced on a branch.

Needle Leaf Soup

A four-year-old
sits in the dirt
beneath the impossibly
tall Norway spruce.
She has a dented pot
and a wooden spoon.

Intuitively she knows
to stir stump water, earth
and fragrant needle
to make her magic.

Parting the Marsh Grass

7

A sandy trail
at the edge of the bay
walks along
the tidal beach -
sometimes there, sometimes not.

It reaches through
the slender
marsh grass
and the hollow reed.

Our feet part
the way and open
a white path
that shines with the night moon.

Birthday Cake

When we were kids,
my brother and I,
mom would slice
the angel food cake
top and bottom.
The base was slathered
with Cool Whip
and a thick layer
of sweet fresh strawberries.

The top half was more lavish.
Strawberries piled so high
they threatened to
(and often did)
tumble to your lap
as you cut
that first spongy piece.

Marbles, Beads and Buttons

9

Three jars on the window sill,
marbles, beads and buttons.
They share the sun
with the rainbow-bent prism
that hangs
on a red satin ribbon.

Dream

It's always difficult
and fraught
with anxiety and doubt.
Highways veer in odd directions.
The unfamiliar and the
faceless roam abandoned
unnamed streets.

Even in a dream
where anything-
everything is possible,
I cannot find my way home.
But every time I wake
two sleeping dogs lie
quietly by my side.

Honeysuckle

A wall of perfume
sweet and seductive
climbs over the brambles
and up the branches.
The scent brings back
days we rode our ponies
bareback, barefoot,
braided with fragrant blooms.

Pinch the green calyx,
slowly pull the style -
one perfect drop
on the tip of the tongue.
Young and sun-drenched
we roamed the fields to
drink the nectar, we became
goddesses on horseback.

Blackberry Cake

Small white-star flowers
brought promise of
Mom's blackberry cake.

Later, in the summer heat,
we picked by the fistful,
filling our buckets while
thorns grabbed our hair
and bloodied our arms.
Would there be a box turtle or
a black snake hidden beneath
the dense thick canes?

She would dredge berries in flour,
fold and bake, then sift
powdered sugar on top -
a dust of sweet to tame the tart.

Orange Dog

The bright orange scotty dog
with rhinestone eyes
is tucked under an arm -
the most coveted place
in a childhood bed.

The other twenty-three,
the pony, the blue cat,
all the assorted animal
menagerie, line the bed
propped against the wall.

There is no sleep without them.
There is no world of infinite
possibility without them.
There is no love ever to be found again
like the love of a stuffed orange dog.

The Mundane and the Profound

As I try to remember
the detail of my dream,
I stand and watch
one specific drop of rain
slide down
the windshield of my car.

One mundane
and profound moment
that only I have witness to
against all of eternity.

It can only be spoken of
within the wet lines
of a poem.

Arrangements

Words fall like leaves
due to mechanisms of nature
and nurture I barely grasp.
I collect them in a basket
and arrange them into
various vases of cut crystal glass.

I humbly present
a bouquet to you -
lines neatly layered
in poetic beat and measure,
punctuated with surprise
and bated breath.

New Goddess

I am interested in a new goddess,
she who knows the
way of the nebula
and the boundaries of the black hole.

The ancient goddesses wrote
awesome scripts for life,
holding the stage through
ages of ignorance and strife.

I'm ready for the next
Mother God, she who slowly
parts the cosmic curtain
with her ancient henna hand.

Between the Lines

17

What does it mean
to stay between the lines
when they refuse to remain
parallel and straight?

I once walked between
two lines that spiraled in
and found myself
in the center of a maze.

What Did You Bring?

18

What did you bring from the hills,
from that house in the holler
from the path that led to the pond?

You brought gifts from
the old world, when
a barefoot path through
the high summer grass
was the known road.

Your gifts are lovely.

River Rock

You have traveled
so far through
heat and ice
to land
in my jacket pocket
to rest on my table.

River Birch

All this week
the river birch trees
have showered tiny
snowflake seeds.
They carpet the yard.

They do not helicopter
like the maple but float,
thin and pale,
choosing to ride
a warm spring breeze.

Wrack Life

21

Driftwood and pebbles tired
of the tidal reach land
on a small brackwater beach.
Old walnuts, sticks,
feathers and bottle tops.
A lone mussel shell,
purple with iridescence.
A bit of broken pier,
a bottle without message.
The wrack of all who live
along miles and miles of bay.

We take the bits and sculpt
a monument in the sand.
A testament to your travels
and your long-forgotten ways.